DATE DUE

Sorting

by Jennifer L. Marks

Capstone press®

Mankato, Minnesota

A+ Books are published by Capstone Press,
151 Good Counsel Drive, P.O. Box 669, Mankato, Minnesota 56002.
www.capstonepress.com

1 2 3 4 5 6 12 11 10 09 08 07

Library of Congress Cataloging-in-Publication Data
Marks, Jennifer L.
     Sorting toys/by Jennifer L. Marks.
     p. cm.—(A+ books. Sorting)
     Summary: "Simple text and color photographs introduce basic ways to sort toys"—Provided by publisher.
     Includes bibliographical references and index.
     ISBN-13: 978-0-7368-6737-5 (hardcover)
     ISBN-10: 0-7368-6737-6 (hardcover)
     ISBN-13: 978-0-7368-7855-5 (softcover pbk.)
     ISBN-10: 0-7368-7855-6 (softcover pbk.)
     1. Group theory—Juvenile literature. 2. Set theory—Juvenile literature. 3. Toys—Juvenile literature. I. Title.
II. Series.
QA174.5M377 2007
512'.2—dc22   2006018256

Credits

Ted Williams, designer; Charlene Deyle, photo researcher; Scott Thoms, photo editor

Photo Credits

Capstone Press/Deirdre Barton, 26; Karon Dubke, cover, 3, 4–5, 6–7, 8, 9, 10, 11, 12–13, 14–15,
     16, 17, 18–19, 20, 21, 22, 23, 24, 25
Index Stock Imagery/Omni Photo Communications Inc., 27 (bottom)
Shutterstock/Alexphoto, 29; Donald Gargano, 28
SuperStock/Dynamic Graphics Value, 27 (top)

Note to Parents, Teachers, and Librarians

The Sorting set uses color photographs and a nonfiction format to introduce readers to the key math
skill of sorting. *Sorting Toys* is designed to be read aloud to a pre-reader, or to be read independently
by an early reader. Images and activities encourage mathematical thinking in early readers and
listeners. The book encourages further learning by including the following sections: Table of Contents,
Venn Diagram, Facts about Toys, Glossary, Read More, Internet Sites, and Index. Early readers may
need assistance using these features.

The author dedicates this book to Mark Sundell of New Ulm, Minnesota.

Table of Contents

Toys, Toys, Toys!

This playroom has lots of toys of all colors, shapes, and sizes.

Let's sort them out. When we put alike toys together, we make sets. What other ways can we sort toys?

Sorting by Color

Creepy, crawly bugs come in lots of colors.

Let's sort these critters into green, blue, yellow, and red sets.

So many cups, pots, and saucers! Let's invite a friend for a tea party.

Before we meet for tea, we sort it all into sets—orange, yellow, and purple.

We can sort building blocks by color too. What color sets do you see here?

13

Sorting by Size

Let's try sorting toys by size. These nesting dolls all look alike. We can sort them, big to little.

Teeth, claws, scales, and tails! Dinosaur toys rule the playroom.

We can sort these dinos by size, shortest to tallest.

A cuddly set of puppies
is sorted by size too—
smallest to biggest.

How Do You Use It?

A cowboy with a magic wand? These dress-up sets are all mixed up.

Let's sort before we start to play—cowboy, pirate, and princess.

Toys can be sorted by where you play. Racetracks, board games, and action figures are for playing indoors.

Bikes, butterfly nets, and footballs are sorted in an outdoor set.

Venn Diagram

Some toys can be sorted into more than one set. Let's see what happens when we sort yellow and purple.

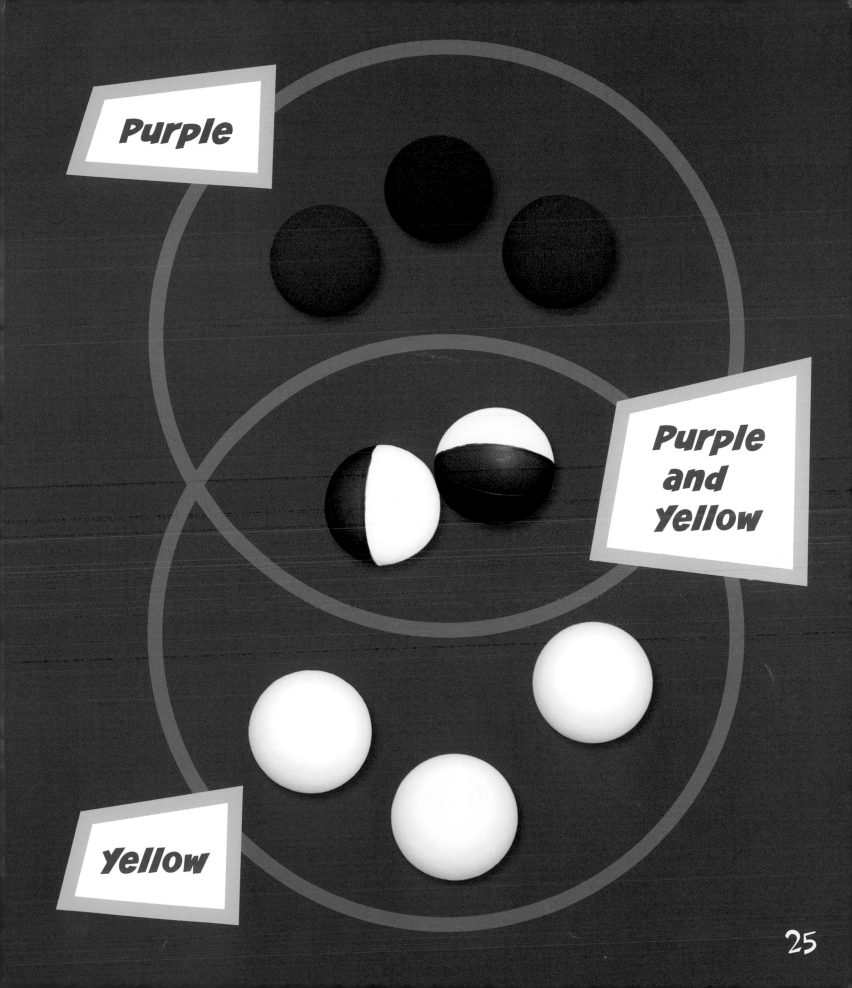

Purple

Purple and Yellow

Yellow

25

Sorting Toys in the Real World

You can spot sorting in all kinds of places. Let's look at some ways people sort toys in the real world.

Fairs and carnivals give away plenty of toys as prizes. The toys are sorted into rows. If you win a game or contest, you get to pick a toy from one of the rows.

School gyms have many kinds of balls. Soccer balls, rubber balls, and basketballs are sorted into bins. Teachers and students can find just what they need to play.

Toy stores have aisles of sorted toys. Each kind of board game has its own place on the store's shelves.

Facts about Toys

- Yo-yos have been around longer than almost any other toy in human history. The oldest yo-yos were discovered in Greece. They were made of stone more than 3,000 years ago.

- Early footballs were much larger than today's footballs. They were shaped kind of like watermelons, so they are often called watermelon footballs. Modern footballs are smaller, and the ends are more pointed. This new style makes them much easier to hold, catch, and throw.

- A set of Russian nesting dolls, or *matryoshka* dolls, may include 5 to 30 dolls that fit one inside another. Each doll is handmade from wood and carefully painted. The dolls are usually made in order, smallest to biggest. The smallest doll cannot be taken apart.

- Checkers is a board game that was around in ancient times in Egypt and other countries. Today, the game is called checkers in the United States and draughts in England.

- The teddy bear was named after United States President Theodore Roosevelt. After one of the president's hunting trips, newspapers started printing cartoons that showed Roosevelt refusing to shoot a bear cub. Toymakers made stuffed versions of the bear cub and called them teddy bears.

Glossary

carnival (KAR-nuh-vuhl)—a public celebration, often with rides and games

critter (KRIT-uhr)—a living creature

nesting doll (NESS-ting DOL)—one of a set of dolls of decreasing sizes placed one inside another

saucer (SAW-sur)—a small, shallow plate that is placed under a cup

set (SET)—a group of similar things

Venn diagram (VEN DYE-uh-gram)—a kind of diagram that uses circles to show how things can belong to more than one set

Read More

Bauer, David. *Let's Sort.* Mankato, Minn.: Yellow Umbrella, 2003.

Kompelien, Tracy. *Let's Sort, It's a Real Sport.* Math Made Fun. Edina, Minn.: Abdo, 2007.

Pluckrose, Henry. *Sorting and Sets.* Let's Explore. North Mankato, Minn.: Sea to Sea, 2006.

Internet Sites

FactHound offers a safe, fun way to find Internet sites related to this book. All of the sites on FactHound have been researched by our staff.

Here's how:

1. Visit *www.facthound.com*

2. Choose your grade level.

3. Type in this book ID **0736867376** for age-appropriate sites. You may also browse subjects by clicking on letters, or by clicking on pictures and words.

4. Click on the **Fetch It** button.

FactHound will fetch the best sites for you!

Index